EVENSONG
quiet songs of hope

Visit Shawnee Press Online at **www.shawneepress.com/songbooks**

GlorySound

EXCLUSIVELY DISTRIBUTED BY

HAL•LEONARD®
CORPORATION

7777 W. BLUEMOUND RD. P.O. BOX 13819 MILWAUKEE, WI 53213

FOREWORD

"…any man can sing in the day, but only God can give songs in the night!"
Charles Spurgeon

When words alone are not enough, music helps speak to the deepest emotions of the heart. Music can comfort the broken spirit and bring solace to the sorrowful. Music can offer consolation to the grieving and bring peace to those who seeking.

In the quiet hush of contemplation, music can decorate our silence with the graceful sounds of assurance. It can awaken in us the dormant memories of hope that rest in the cloistered chapels of our heart. God's music strengthens and affirms our life and encourages our journey of faith.

As you play and share these timeless songs of promise, may you be surrounded by the gentle music of God's love and may the echoes of your playing ring peace to all who hear it.

The Publisher

Going Home

African-American Spiritual

Arranged by
JOSEPH M. MARTIN (BMI)

'TIS SO SWEET TO TRUST IN JESUS

Tune: **TRUST IN JESUS**
By WILLIAM J. KIRKPATRICK
Arranged by
VICKI TUCKER COURTNEY

His Eye Is On The Sparrow

Words by
CIVILLA D. MARTIN (1869-1948)

Music by
CHARLES H. GABRIEL (1856-1932)

Arranged by
MARK HAYES (ASCAP)

Moderately, with expression

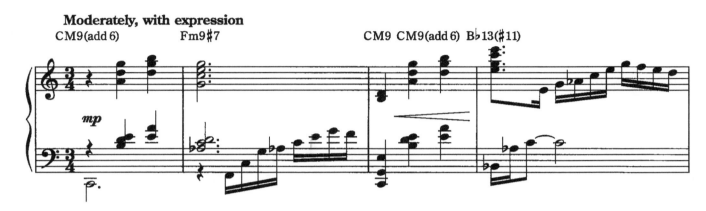

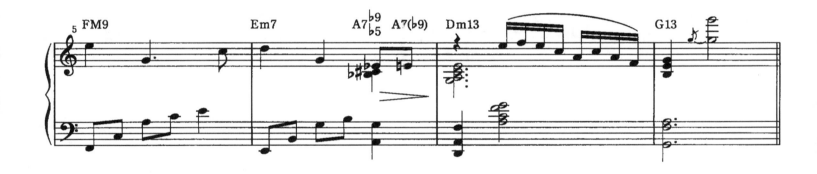

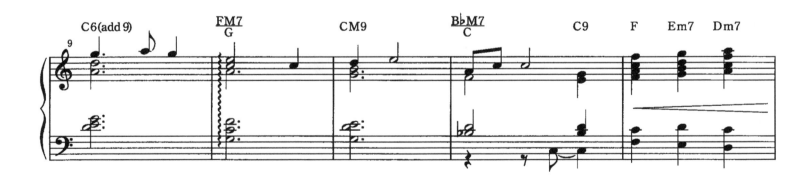

The Lord's My Shepherd, I'll Not Want

with "Savior, Like a Shepherd Lead Us"

CRIMOND (Jessie S. Irvine)
BRADBURY (William B. Bradbury)
Arranged by LLOYD LARSON (ASCAP)

Fairest Lord Jesus

Arranged by ERIC DAUB

CRUSADERS' HYMN (ST. ELIZABETH)

Slowly, freely

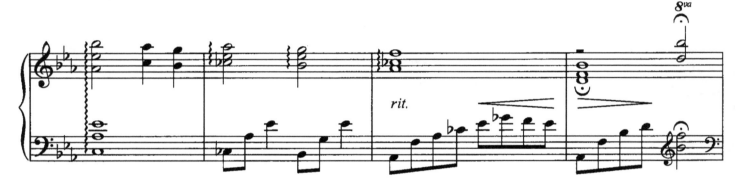

a tempo

Steady tempo (♩ = ca. 90)

in fond memory of Pastor W. Ted Harmon

Face to Face

with "Saved by Grace" — George Stebbins (1846-1945)

Arranged by LARRY SHACKLEY (ASCAP)

GRANT C. TULLAR
(1869-1950)

KUM BA YAH, MY SHEPHERD

Tunes: **KUM BA YAH,** African Folk Song
and **RESIGNATION,** Traditional American Hymn
Arranged by SHARON ELERY ROGERS

for KayLynn Moltmann

NEARER, STILL NEARER

Music by LELIA N. MORRIS
Arranged by
SHIRLEY BRENDLINGER*

* Compositional style based on Robert Schumann's *Romance, Op. 28*.

Tranquillo

pp

to Tracey Martin

Improvisation on
"Balm In Gilead"

Traditional Spiritual

Arranged by
JOSEPH M. MARTIN (BMI)

I Am His, and He Is Mine
(Nocturne)

Tune: *Everlasting Love*
by James Mountain, c. 1890

Arranged by
CINDY BERRY (ASCAP)

I WILL ARISE AND GO TO JESUS

Tune: **RESTORATION**
Walker's Southern Harmony
Arranged by
HEATHER SORENSON

Rubato, with feeling (♩ = ca. 124-130)

SERENITY

SUSAN BUCKLEY CUMBIE (ASCAP)

with much expression

as in the beginning

p

MEDITATION ON CANDLER

Tune: **CANDLER**
Traditional Scottish Melody
Arranged by
VICKI COLLINSWORTH

Gently flowing (♪ = ca. 132)

mp

Pedal carefully throughout.

more movement

f

for Tiffany Barclay

MY JESUS, I LOVE THEE

Tune: **GORDON**
By ADONIRAM J. GORDON
Arranged by
SHIRLEY BRENDLINGER*

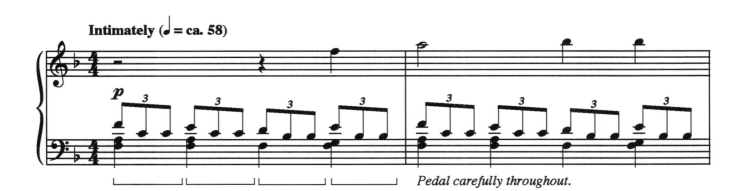

Intimately (♩ = ca. 58)

Pedal carefully throughout.

Expressively

* Inspired by Frederic Chopin's *Nocturne, op. 15, #1*.

GOD LEADS US ALONG

G.A. YOUNG
Arranged by
JAMES M. STEVENS

ALL THROUGH THE NIGHT

Tune: **AR HYD Y NOS**
Traditional Welsh Melody
Arranged by
HEATHER SORENSON

* *Tune*: **Country Gardens** by Percy Grainger

The Road Home

JOSEPH M. MARTIN (BMI)

EXCITING KEYBOARD COLLECTIONS

THE BEST OF MARK HAYES VOLUME 2
by Mark Hayes

The Best of Mark Hayes Volume 2 is a follow-up to the smashing success of his inaugural compilation. This potpourri of praise from the renowned composer and performer is a must for every pianist. This stellar second volume focuses on contemporary classics arranged with that unmistakable Mark Hayes touch. There are several selections written especially for this collection making this an essential and permanent addition to your keyboard library.

Contains: **Great Is Thy Faithfulness • People Need the Lord • How Majestic Is Your Name • In Christ Alone • Sing to the Lord • The Light of the World Is Jesus • Praise His Greatness • He Giveth More Grace/No One Ever • Sing Hallelujah • Alfred Burt Carol Medley • Resurrection Medley • Pass It On • Interlude • The Love of Jesus Medley • I'd Rather Have Jesus**

HE5142 • Piano Collection • $24.95
GN6025 • Book/CD Combo • $29.95
ND6023 • Listening CD
(Features Mark Hayes at the keyboard) • $15.98

The Original Best-Selling Collection!
THE BEST OF MARK HAYES
Arranged by Mark Hayes
HE5137 • Piano Collection • $19.95
GN6010 • Book/CD Combo • $24.95
ND6010 • Listening CD • $15.98

BEST-SELLING KEYBOARD RESOURCES

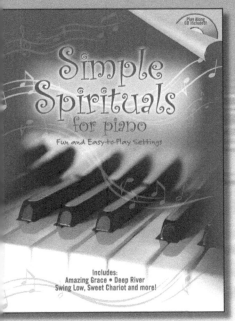

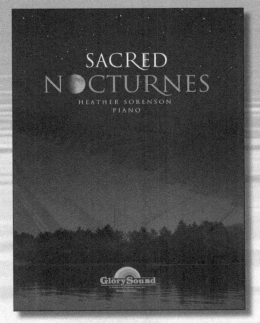

SIMPLE SPIRITUALS FOR PIANO
Fun and Easy-to-Play Settings

Features a play-along CD with demonstration performances.

Includes: **Amazing Grace • Down By the Riverside • He's Got the Whole World in His Hands • Peace Like a River • Steal Away • Swing Low Sweet Chariot • Wade in the Water •** and more

SB1034 • Piano Collection/CD • $16.95

SACRED NOCTURNES
by Heather Sorenson

Church pianists everywhere will want to play these beautiful arrangements during offertories, communion and other special events.

Includes: **I Will Arise and Go to Jesus • Be Thou My Vision • This Is My Father's World • Shall We Gather at the River • Be Still My Soul • Nearer, My God, To Thee • Turn Your Eyes Upon Jesus • 'Til We Meet Again •** and more

HE5140 • Piano Book • $18.95
ND6020 • Enhanced Listening CD
(with bonus PDF material) • $16.95
GN6022 • Piano Book • $16.95

MORE JAZZED ON HYMNS

A piano collection of classic hymns in a light jazz style, featuring a CD with play-along tracks and printable chord charts.

Includes: **Crown Him With Many Crowns • It Is Well With My Soul • I Surrender • For the Beauty of the Earth •** and more

SB1039 • Piano Collection/CD • $22.95

Available from your favorite music supplier.   Prices and availability subject to change without notice.